The Potential of a Puddle

Mind Stretchers™

For our Emily
Many thanks to all the children and adults who have made this book possible.
All that is left is for you to take this book outside, find a space, sit and read !!

ISBN 095448835 - 0

If you would like training materials or inservice on this book, please contact Mindstretchers.

Mindstretchers
The Warehouse
Rossie Place
Auchterarder
Perthshire
PH3 1AJ

Tel/Fax: 01764 664409
www.mindstretchers.co.uk

Contents

Foreword

Whatever your expertise in Early Years outdoor practice, this book will help you. For those who find excuses that block progress in developing a good learning environment that links with indoors, this book will demolish the negative attitudes. It is full of ideas to motivate and to allow the practitioner's own imagination to take flight – I was particularly keen on the section where we were encouraged to be a dung beetle! But high-quality outdoor play does not come without rigorous planning and skilled adult interactions with children. This book argues strongly for practitioners to put in place all the conditions that will make outdoor learning enjoyable and exciting for children and adults alike.

The title alone will ensure that the book will make a big splash with everyone who reads it!

Marjorie Ouvry
Consultant in Early Years Education

Introduction

The real value of outdoor play is derived through striking a balance between an outdoor learning environment and an area for the sheer fun of moving.

Warden (1999)

The curriculum for the early years is structured by the guidelines laid down in the documents 'A Curriculum Framework for Children in their Pre-school Year' published by the Scottish Office (1997), 'Nursery Education Desirable Outcomes for Children's Learning' in England and Wales, and the 'enriched curriculum' in Northern Ireland. All of these documents view learning as holistic, that is, it develops in an integrated way across all areas of the curriculum, with links helping to further understanding. Rather than being receivers of information, young children need to enjoy the experience of discovery, so

that they can apply knowledge, concepts and skills, and take calculated risks in a structured rather than a directed environment. In all activities, children need to **play**.

In the key aspect of physical development and movement, the statement 'children should enjoy physical development indoors and out' is enough justification to consider the role of the outdoor environment in the learning process. The outdoor environment is, however, far more than a place to move. All aspects of an early years curriculum should be explored outdoors. Outdoor play contains many valuable

'Exploring the potential of a puddle'

opportunities for learning and development that are unique to it, such as the interaction with nature, multi-sensory learning that evolves and changes over time, a sense of freedom, and of course fresh air.

'Learning to explore together'

This document looks at the principles and key features that underlie good use of the outdoor environment for play. The first part of the document outlines the unique benefits that children derive from play in a high-quality outdoor environment. The second part of the document identifies nine principles that are essential for fostering effective learning in an outdoor environment. The third part of the document gives some case study examples from centres across Scotland where these principles have been put into practice.

'All children enjoy being outside'

Adult interaction in the learning process, and adult structuring of learning, affect the way that children engage in learning. The way that we work with young children, both indoors and outdoors, is therefore of paramount importance. This document looks at the methodology of working in an outdoor environment.

'The wonder of nature'

'Look at things from a different perspective !'

Because different areas have their own landscape architecture, building layout and accessibility, there are few that meet everyone's criteria of a perfect outdoor area for children's learning. Some centres have small play areas of tarmac that have been transformed into havens for children to explore, other centres have large outdoor areas with basic landscaping and are now looking at how the area is used by the children and staff. Everyone is in a process of development and change; it is just that some centres are further along a development route than others.

For development to take place, we need to motivate parents, carers and practitioners from all aspects of education – staff in educare centres and baby units, childminders, and nursery staff – to see the magic of outdoor play.

It is human nature to put up barriers to change; indeed it is often an easier option to maintain the status quo. Practitioners can identify many issues that they feel conspire to reduce the amount of time spent outside:

·   shared play areas with the rest of the primary school
·   the need for staffing and supervision of the outdoor area
·   the weather
·   parental attitude to outdoor play
·   lack of enthusiasm from the children
·   an area with limited resources – 'only muddy grass'
·   unwelcome or dangerous litter such as glass and needles
·   too far to walk to get outside
·   the need to cross car parks to get to a bit of grass
·   lack of a climbing frame
·   not enough bikes
·   no storage.

'Everything has got potential !'

The list can seem overwhelming, although it would be useful to reflect on which of the issues above are real barriers to outdoor play, and which are used by adults as excuses. We need to see the potential in every area for outdoor play.

We have some way to go before *all* children in Scotland are able to access high-quality learning outdoors for long periods of time. It is hoped that this document will enthuse practitioners to find a pathway through the obstacles in their own location, so that the outdoor play area and the way it is used are improved in even the smallest way. This document will give examples of good practice in environments that are not ideal, it will show how much can be achieved through

'Wall art'

collaboration and team effort and it will discuss small changes and large-scale developments with all the advantages and challenges that they offer.

Outdoor experiential learning has been a part of many societies and cultures for a long time. There are good examples of practice from around the world that could

'Stimuli can come from the most surprising places !'

be explored, but there is enough excellent practice in Scotland to celebrate in this document. In Scotland we have overtaken the challenges of area layout, rather high rainfall, and even midges, to create some very effective learning environments for the young children in our care.

Why should children go out of doors?

Given all the apparent challenges, why do we still persist in the promotion of play in a high-quality outdoor environment?
What unique benefits can children gain out of doors?

A sense of freedom

Many children lead 'organised' and often sedentary lives, whether indoors sitting at a computer or a television, at a club, or in a car. The freedom that many of us felt in our youth is being curtailed by highly structured experiences in enclosed environments that are usually indoors. Children need a sense of autonomy if they are to develop a belief in themselves. Effective outdoor play provides a greater sense of freedom: for example the opportunity to make a large-scale structure that *you* want to hide in, a project that *you* want to develop over a series of days, using *your* own choice of materials, is full of emotional learning.

'Freedom'

Freedom can be expressed through the amount of time provided, the space the children can access and the choice of resources.

Experiencing the weather

Human beings are part of nature, but many children and adults have become removed from it. Nature is often conveniently packaged or sanitised so that we experience it only from inside a car, or on a walkway through a wood.

'Connecting with nature'

Young children have a natural connectedness to nature: their joy of standing in a puddle or watching a worm move is central to their understanding of who they are in the world. Instead of presenting nature in packages, we need to follow young children and engage in more experiences to *feel* it. Experiencing the weather is the one totally unique aspect of outdoor play. Children naturally move in an environment that is constantly changing from minute to minute and from season to season. These changes create an exciting space to play. Light changes, casting shadows and patterns of coloured light; the wind moves objects both fixed and free; the rain makes the world a shiny place with light bouncing off surfaces that previously looked dull.

Sensorial learning that changes with the seasons

The sensory aspects of natural environments provide unique opportunities for learning outdoors. We now know a great deal about the way that learning takes place in the brain, and the sensorium is the part of the brain in which sensations take place. We all learn in different ways and have a preferred learning style. Plastic materials are widely used in centres to motivate young children, but they engage mainly

visual learners. Sensory materials such as grass, leaves, water, mud, wood and rock all naturally occur in a well designed outdoor area. The sensorial experience of nature ensures that we feel the wind, smell the grass, hear the bird song, see the colours change and sometimes eat the carrots that we have grown.

Learning through movement

Children need to have space to be able to move with speed, to run, climb, balance and skip. The physical mastery of the body is important for the reinforcement of the neural pathways in the brain that are connected to all aspects of learning. Children need to be stimulated by movement, whether through watching objects such as wind-socks, trees, kites or feathers blowing in the wind; through sitting on moving objects such as swings; or through controlling the movement of their own bodies.

Developing a positive attitude towards the world we live in: citizenship

Involving children in the design, creation and care of the outdoor environment is an excellent and meaningful way of developing the skills and knowledge required to

become caring and responsible citizens. For example, children can create small arable fields, then tend the plants with care and concern, from the first planting to the harvesting of the crop. Experiential learning has been a model used in early education for some time, because it is effective. Watering plants, digging, handling mini-beasts or sweeping leaves are all behaviours that have an emotional connection to a child

Potential of a puddle

and are more likely to stay with them into adulthood.

Involving children as partners in the learning process ensures that both adult and child see the outdoor area as a place for learning and teaching, a shared two-way process.

Experiencing biodiversity

The Earth is a wonderful place full of a variety of life. Some children have a limited access to this dimension due to the place that they live. Totally concrete zones make it difficult to develop an admiration for the wonderment of nature. Parks offer spaces, but the opportunities for digging to find a worm, or to pick flowers so that you can take them apart, are limited. If children are going to look after the world they live in they first need to be aware of it, to come to admire it and ultimately to care for it. Given time nature does re-establish itself in all our environments, plants grow out of cracks in the rock, sediment around a drain provides a place for a wild flower to live. With a little help all outside areas can encourage nature to come back in.

'Exploring nature's light'

One nursery planted Dandelions, Couch grass, Daisies and Dock leaves in plastic hanging bags and put them on the fence, the plants were robust enough to be handled and used. When the children made designs for a more permanent area, these plants featured as their favourites. The outdoor learning environment can be developed into a miniature version of environments that we have in the world: a seashore with shells, a forest zone, a freshwater pond with frogs. These give a positive experience of biodiversity and our effect on it. In reality the shells may be in a sandpit, the forest may be a few trees and the freshwater pond a puddle, but children will still become more aware and more informed critical thinkers about our relationship with the natural world around us.

Becoming environmentally aware

Many early years centres have developed links with eco-school projects taking place across Scotland. The project focuses on sustainability and how to have a more environmentally friendly lifestyle. It explores ecological issues, including waste management, such as re-cycling, litter, health and well-being. It also looks at transport e.g. travelling to school, water, energy and of course the outdoor environment. One of the key elements to the eco-school development is the creation of pupil councils that are made up from all the participants. Members include parents, pupils from all ages, and staff. The council is democratic and issues are identified through consultation with the whole centre/school.

Consultation is very important throughout all aspects of education if change is to be embedded in practice. The materials that we use for outdoor play can give children clear messages about re-cycling and more environmentally friendly ways of working. Using old envelopes and paper to make palm-sized books for writing outside, creating bug mats from old carpet squares, or flower beds/sand pits from old tyres are all practical examples of helping children to be eco-friendly. The outdoor space can be used to explore more global issues such as energy conservation and sources. Introduce solar power through rainbow makers on the window, powered pebble pools, movable solar lights for winter evenings or a mobile power pack to allow the use of a variety of technology from inside the centre.

When nursery gardens were first set up they were used to provide extra food in the post war years. The process of growing and tending plants still engages children although a separate area for digging is recommended. Growing objects can be done through hydroponics (water fed systems), or drip filters (hose pipe with holes in it to allow the water to dribble out either on the garden , in tubs or in a water play area), and through management of water supplies through the use of containers with taps. Simple gardens can be made with potagers (Warden 1999) that allow children to reach all areas to dig and tend.

Compost bins and wormeries are being introduced in many eco-schools and centres so that children can see the way that their food waste is transformed into soil.

Early years centres have always been good at re-using materials. The outdoor space is a perfect place to use some of the larger items that are now classed as 'urban waste'. Milk crates are rare now with the increase in containers, so bottle crates are as good. Use the tetra pak containers to create birdfeeders. Tubing used for the protection of cables underground comes in a variety of diameters and colours. They are not 100% UV stable so they will need to be replaced at regular intervals. Real cones for roadway use, barriers and hazard tapes. The real objects really are the best. By reusing objects and re-cycling as much as we can, we are trying to reduce the size of the environmental footprint that we leave on the earth in our lifetime. Children can work in a contextual way to develop environmental awareness in a positive way.

Enjoyment

Last, but not least, being outside offers all children a great sense of joy. In a well-structured outdoor environment, children engage themselves physically in learning about all aspects of the curriculum. It is clear that outdoor learning is especially beneficial to young children who are bodily kinaesthetic learners; these children need to learn through activity and do not learn well in environments where space is restricted or opportunities for learning are seat-based. An outdoor learning programme is well suited to the way these children learn and can often transform behaviour.

Enjoyment

Potential of a puddle

Creating effective environments for outdoor learning

This part of the book examines the principles and key features that contribute to the creation of effective outdoor learning environments for young children. These principles are based on observations of, and information gathered from, staff teams across Scotland.

These nine principles have been identified as essential to effective outdoor learning. They are the feature that make the difference between an area that is satisfactory to one that is excellent, "The added value".

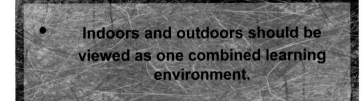
Indoors and outdoors should be viewed as one combined learning environment.

Outdoor areas should be resourced in a flexible way.

Planning should support learning in an outdoors environment.

Parents, carers and children should all be involved.

Potential of a puddle

- Outdoor play should receive the same management as indoor play.

- Practitioners should be committed to children learning in an outdoor environment.

- The physical aspects of the outdoor area should be addressed creatively.

- Practitioners should be aware of the range of children's learning styles and preferences.

- Staff should develop a policy so that they have a common understanding of, and a consistent approach to, outdoor learning.

Each of these nine principles is analysed in the following sections.

Potential of a puddle

Indoors and outdoors should be viewed as one combined learning environment

Key points

· The curriculum should be addressed across both indoor and outdoor areas so that specific aspects do not need to be replicated in each area.

· There should be access to both indoor and outdoor areas at the same time so that there can be a flow of ideas and resources.

· Substantial time needs to be given to children playing out of doors so that a depth of learning can take place.

· The ethos of a combined learning environment should be reflected in a single planning process/policy. (Page 37)

The environment clearly has a direct effect on how and what young children learn. Children can learn from direct teaching through the interaction with someone else, or through their environment by means of discovery. Bruce (1987, p. 54) argues that 'the environment is the mechanism by which the teacher brings the child and different areas of knowledge together'. Discovery and self-enquiry are important methods of learning and should not be seen as secondary to direct teaching. If discovery learning is important it should not be left completely to chance. The environment should be structured so that key opportunities are available to children to enable discoveries to take place. The outdoor environment has to be planned carefully so that it has the same status, although different features, as the indoor environment.

"McDonalds' for dinosaurs'

Outdoor play is often viewed as an activity that receives little structure, especially in terms of adult interaction. Many children are left to 'get on with it' with little thought to teaching and learning. Moyles (1992) argues that teachers have to decide what to teach and what to leave for children to find out on their own. Encouraging children to learn through discovery suggests that there is little or no adult input, but this is not the case; an adult should be nearby to *support* the learning. The difference lies in the fact that the adult role is not dominant.

The environment as an educator

Adult inter-action

11

The view of the outdoor area as an area of equal importance means that the learning opportunities offered indoors do not need to be replicated outdoors, and vice versa. In centres where children cannot move easily between an indoor area and an outdoor area, the initial framework/structure for learning may well come from the adults to ensure breadth and balance. In centres that are fortunate enough to have an environment with free flow between indoor and outdoor areas, it is possible to create links that are easy to manage. However, even in these centres, the physical layout has to be supported by the practitioners working within it.

'Plans & designs'

Tipi based experiences linked to design work inside the nursery that could then be linked to outdoor structure building.

Any type of learning takes time, especially projects that involve building, growth, experimentation and discovery. Allocating substantial time to outdoor learning will enable children to re-visit, test, fail, succeed and reflect so that there is a greater depth of learning.

'Connecting & joining'

The implicit messages contained in planning sheets and policies often convey the value given to an area of the curriculum. Where outdoor play is included as an extra column on planning sheets, it suggests that this activity is seen as outside the main learning. The planning sheet should include opportunities for learning that takes place both indoors and outdoors, with clear learning links between the two.

Outdoor areas should be resourced in a flexible way

Key points

· Children should be able to change and modify the outdoor area according to their needs.

· Children should be provided with systems that enable them to carry and combine resources easily and take part in creating and packing away the outdoor learning area.

· Open-ended resources should be provided that can be used in a variety of ways to support different activities.

· Large permanent structures need to be examined carefully for their learning potential.

Flexibility provides opportunities for autonomy and creative thought. Children are often presented with resources and games that have been made to an adult design. We need to consider the resources we provide and the layout of the outdoor area to monitor what degree of learning has been removed from children through adult intervention at any point in the resource development.

Most centres have experienced occasions where an adult has intervened in children's outdoor learning with the best of intentions, but has suddenly changed the atmosphere and direction of the play. Some children stop altogether and stand and watch, while the adult takes the lead and makes all the decisions. This ability to assume 'learned helplessness' often occurs at points where children feel challenged, through a change in the dynamics of power, or are unsure of their role and autonomy.

'Transient art - Art Attack'

The grouping of resources or the creation of interest bays in the outdoor space will have an effect on the learning that takes place within them. For example, children can create large water runs with no more than guttering, tape and a range of containers such as milk crates; they can use resources to make mud pies or to simulate a fish and chip shop. But the provision of these resources has to be managed properly. Nash (1981) examined the effect

Interest bays

13

of spatially created environments where resources provided are 'linked' so that children can make useful selections and choices.

This works much better than a randomly arranged area where resources such as paper are often presented in separate units. In the latter case children did not link and blend the use of the resources at all.

Self help management systems

Providing linked resources has a direct influence on the way that we present choices and options in outdoor environments. In terms of the sensory aspects of natural outdoor environments, the resource choices are already there. However, in outdoor areas where all the resources have to be carried out from indoors we should consider a system that supports the idea of choice and selection. Teets (1985) found that where children could modify their environment by using combinations of creative materials, dramatic materials and smaller manipulative objects, the quality of play was high.

'We-Go' system

Many of us have clear memories of using 'bits and pieces' as children to create dens. Sheets, blankets and a bit of rope made a den that was left up for play over several days. The skills of working out what area of fabric to use, how to attach it, how taut to make the rope so that it did not slacken, how to anchor the sheet at the base. All these questions require investigative skills and thinking in order to build the den. If we offer even greater challenges such as a basket of a

Open-ended resources

range of types of fabrics to choose from, some heavy, others light, some with holes or waterproof, some absorbent we will increase the challenge and experimentation. The easiest option would be to hand over a pop up tent; the highest quality learning will come from them making it themselves.

If we provide open-ended resources in a way that presents choices and self-selection, children will extend and develop their play in response.

'Sensory experiences with sand'

'Ice sculpture'

Potential of a puddle

Planning should support learning in an outdoor environment

Key points

· Links should be made between indoor and outdoor learning.

· Planning needs to be responsive and flexible so that experiences can be linked to the weather.

· Planning should enable children to progress at a rate that allows them depth of learning.

· Observations and discussions with children should take place to create an effective match between the children's interests, needs and the children's provision.

'Looking at artwork'

There are a number of ways of planning and many styles of planning sheet, so the choices can be overwhelming; here we look only at the way that outdoor learning is integrated into the planning process. The key in terms of effective learning is how the planning informs practice and how children can have ownership of their learning.

Consulting children

The process of consulting children throughout the learning process has been important to many practitioners for some years. Talking and Thinking books © (C. Warden 2005) are an example of a formalised way of valuing children's talk, and these can work very well in linking indoor and outdoor environments. Small groups of children work with an adult scribe to record their thoughts and ideas about a complex issue or project such as 'What is inside a seed?' 'Where do rainbows come from?' 'What kind of den shall we build out of recycled things?' The adult scribes verbatim the children's responses, children can also write in the books, adults can include Mind maps®, children can draw diagrams and pictures, and photographs can be included. The end result reflects the process of learning and practitioners can demonstrate through the planning process how they extended children's existing understanding. Examples such as the talking and thinking book reflect the importance of children's thoughts and ideas, rather than adult-

'Creating towers inside'

'Creating towers outside'

generated opportunities. Children have wonderful, creative ways of looking at learning. The following ideas for outdoor activities came from children who had clear ideas about what they wanted to do.

"Make a home for a wounded frog" (a red permanent marker was used to mark a plastic frog, which was put into a puddle in the tarmac with dock leaves for a bed).

"Make a whirly bit for children to blow, away from the wind." (ribbons of different lengths were tied to a fence and then covered with a flap of wood).

"Build a chute for water to trickle down, not too fast" (guttering was used for the water chute, with fabric placed inside which slowed down the water).

"Make coloured magic water" (three water containers with taps were used, holding red, blue and yellow water, so that when you fill white cups from the taps the water mixes and makes magic colours).

Be a dung beetle (a large piece of tweed fabric was fixed around shoulders; there was space to move fast and then stop, and time to explore the role).

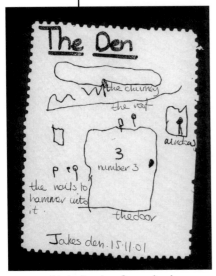
'Jake's plan for a den'

In some cases individual designs can be incorporated into a final product that can be created for the children to use.

In a nursery centre in North Lanarkshire staff use the ideas generated from the Talking and Thinking books © to inform the planning process in response to children's interests. For example, one group wanted to put up a den in the outdoor area. They were provided with a wide range of images to look at. The children then drew their ideas as plans and diagrams, with each child contributing something to the finished design. The den was to have an uneven window with a blue flap on it, a hole for a Christmas tree light cable to go in, three chimneys, and a home for a pet spider in the corner. These ideas were given to a local carpenter who built a den incorporating all the features. (See examples of practice - page 49).

The role of the practitioner here was to facilitate learning through provision of resources, time and space. She enabled children to have ownership of a building that will now be permanent. These children covered all the aspects of the 3–5 curriculum through an outdoor context that mattered to them; there was an emotional link to learning.

'Mind mapping/brainstorms'

Potential of a puddle

Parents, carers and children should all be involved

Key points

· Adults need to see outdoor play as an integral part of early learning.

· Cultural diversity should be celebrated inside and out.

· Appropriate clothing enables people to engage in outdoor learning.

· Parents and carers need to be supported in understanding the learning behind their children's active outdoor play.

When older people are asked the question 'What did you do outside when you were young?', many say that they made their own amusement. They speak fondly of making mud pies, petal perfume, sliding down the 'Bing' on a tin tray, or playing at fish and chip shops using dock leaves. They clearly had a love of being out of doors that transcended the rain. However, often when younger parents are asked the same question they say that they didn't go out, they went to organised clubs instead.

'Chatting under an apple tree'

The magic of being out of doors, the wonderment of seeing your wellies disappear into mud, or of building a grass wall for your own design of house, has been lost from many children's lives and those of their parents. Rather than seeing outdoor play as beneficial and integral to learning, some adults and children view it as something to be endured. Our role in outdoor play is often to bring back the wonderment and magic.

Many parents bring their children by car to our centres and are removed from the feeling of being outside, so children enter our centres with inappropriate clothing for outdoor play. Rather than being critical of this, however, we should try to introduce parents and carers to the benefits of outdoor experiences.

A parent of a child at a nursery recently shared a poem she had written about not having a car to drive to nursery in. The poem spoke about the frustration of walking in the pouring rain pushing a buggy with a child who wanted to jump in the

Parents and carers

'A family drumming workshop in the tipi'

puddles, and of the stress involved in worrying about being late. The poem ended with the joy she felt when she reflected on the warmth they met on arrival at the nursery, and the conversations and laughter they had shared on their journey together. This parent discovered the benefits of outdoor learning by herself. Some parents and carers find written communication more accessible, others enjoy playing with children in the outdoor area, watching videos that talk about the benefits of outdoor learning, annotated photographic displays, or home link programmes that encourage outdoor activity.

Clothing

'Peering out on a foggy day'

The provision of suitable waterproof clothing is critical to the comfort of both adults and children. Given a limited budget, dungarees are the most appropriate form of protection since most children naturally tend to kneel, crouch on the ground, or splash in puddles. If the outdoor area is to be treated in the same way as the indoor area, the centre should provide suitable outdoor clothing, in the same way that water aprons and painting overalls are provided for indoors. Given the amount of rainfall that we have in Scotland, even on dry days there is likely to be a damp area somewhere – and children are bound to find it! Releasing children (and staff) from the concern of dirty clothing will improve interaction and the degree of involvement in outdoor play.

Perceptions

Involving parents in the creation of an outdoor area can be beneficial for everyone. Concerns about dirt, or catching colds, stem from misunderstanding. Short of sending out a letter from the local GP, a conversation will always be the most effective way of dealing with this.

Children's ideas of what they like to see in outdoor spaces are covered elsewhere in this book. Parents and carers need to be supported in understanding the learning behind their children's ideas of a mud puddle, or a ramp with small bricks on it, or a sunflower tunnel.

There are occasions when the subtle messages we convey to visitors speak volumes about the importance we place on things. Although time spent observing children is important, a visitor who sees a group of staff sitting on deckchairs chatting may well come to the conclusion that outdoor play is no more than a play time. Staff interaction and an active purposeful outdoor space will convey a clear message that children do learn effectively inside or out.

Implicit messages

'Picnic in the woods'

18

Potential of a puddle

Outdoor play should receive the same management as indoor play

Key points

- Staff:child ratios should be appropriate for the indoor /outdoor balance of learning.

- Outdoor space should be subdivided to create a range of areas that can be modified by children.

- Outdoor experiences should be child-led with the adult facilitating the learning, rather than directing one activity.

- There should be flexible timetabling/time spent outside.

- Resources should be presented in a self-help way to mirror the methodology used indoors.

- Children should be able to choose from a range of cross-curricular resources.

There are two issues that underlie the staffing of outdoor areas: the method/cost of maintaining appropriate staff:child ratios; and the management of outdoor learning areas by staff. Decisions about how to staff outdoor areas will be affected by the way the area can be accessed. Some centres allocate a number of staff to the total space, and the staff come and go from outdoors as required. Other centres allocate specific staff to the outdoor learning area for a period of time such as a month. Others plan outdoor learning, and its staff supervision, as a separate activity: for example, some centres have key groups going outdoors at set times, no matter what the weather.

'Easter tree in the playground'

In each case, risk must be monitored carefully; safety is a way of life, not a paper exercise. Staff working outdoors should carry a hip pouch with emergency first aid, and also a way of communicating with staff indoors, such as a walkie-talkie or a mobile phone. They may also want to look after resources that require supervision, such as scissors; and paper for

Staff child ratios

Adult interaction

Risk assessment

Designing plant pots

observation notes etc. Staff working outdoors should be on the move and therefore the resources should be portable too.

The creation of a range of outdoor spaces that can be modified by children will help to support a balance of independent (free-flow) play and adult-initiated activities. This will enable staff to work effectively using observations and interactions to move children's learning forward. Too many adult-initiated activities will challenge even the most effective staff teams.

In most centres the ethos is that children's learning should flow over time barriers such as days and blocks of segmented time. This should be true of outdoor play as well as indoor learning. The strict timetabling that gives children a 15-minute block outdoors can be seen to be more like school playtime, with issues surrounding the type and quality of play. The behaviour observed in centres where

'Sound' area

children know they have only a short time outdoors is more frantic; children rarely settle. When the time spent outside is longer, and there is an understanding that projects started one day will continue over a series of days, the behaviour is more engaged and often leads to a greater depth of learning. Centres that are at risk of vandalism and need to clear away outdoor structures at the end of each day can use digital cameras to take pictures of structures built outdoors. This enables children to clear away structures at the end of the day and quickly re-build them next day.

Children benefit from making their own selection from a wide range of resources, covering all aspects of the curriculum. Starting points come from children and take learning forward in a holistic way.

Discovering a snail

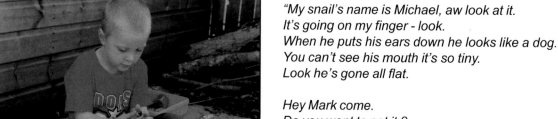

"My snail's name is Michael, aw look at it.
It's going on my finger - look.
When he puts his ears down he looks like a dog.
You can't see his mouth it's so tiny.
Look he's gone all flat.

Hey Mark come.
Do you want to pat it ?
Be really gentle.
Courtney - come and see this
Is it a snake ?
No it's a snail"

Example of talking to friends about observations

Practitioners should be committed to children learning in an outdoor environment

Key points

· Practitioners make the most impact on the development and sustainability of outdoor learning environments.

· Practitioners' personal beliefs and strengths can be the most powerful motivation.

· Practitioners' should be knowledgable and informed about outdoor play and learning

The staff role in an outdoor learning environment is integral to its success. Although planning can be put into place, the environment organised, and the children present, it is the ongoing commitment and enthusiasm of the staff to learning out of doors that will ensure its sustainability. McLean (1991) refers to the effective adult as going through a process of fine tuning on a continual basis. This describes the role well: to observe children, analyse their learning and respond to it while still maintaining a curricular focus is one of the skills of being an early years facilitator. The people who have this skill have developed a view of learning that takes it away from the tabletop to a mobile, experiential process, and are able to identify learning in all its forms.

Adult role

'Staff working at a child's level'

This fine tuning can involve the removal or addition of resources to widen the play or to re-direct it: for example, introducing more binoculars, a blanket and pegs for children to create an observation den; creating intangible boundaries to enable learning to take place by supporting uncertain children or overzealous ones; providing hidden treasures to extend the involvement in the treasure hunt. It requires a high level of perception to anticipate needs and events before they occur.

The need to tidy up outdoor areas can often come in the way of learning; outdoor play is a creative process and usually generates mess. Muddy puddles, guttering and milk crates are not pleasing to some adult eyes. There should be a balance of when to clear up and when not to. The Gura (1992) study suggested that block play

Creativity

21

stopped when the area became too chaotic. The same is true of outdoor learning; if areas become too chaotic, with guttering coming in the way of mud pies and a ball hitting the pot, the play will become frustrating for children. Creating an expectation of playing then clearing away in a series of waves would seem to be the most flexible approach rather than clearing up every 15 minutes and moving on to another activity.

'Interaction throughout session'

Intrinsic motivation comes with personal rewards. Practitioners who believe that children benefit from being outdoors will ensure that children are given that opportunity every day, regardless of the weather. Obstructions to outdoor learning, such as vandalism, space, layout and resources, should be seen as challenges rather than reasons to give up.

The gender balance of many staff teams is towards female dominance, which carries with it some of the stereotypical roles of our society. Although females are becoming more outdoor focused, many do not find it a natural place to work. Tizard (1977) found that there were significant differences in the way staff worked indoors and out of doors. The interaction and cognitive challenges were sometimes lower out of doors, whereas the 'safety type' of interaction ('slow down on that bike') increased.

Gender balance

One of our challenges as practitioners is to question the stereotypes, so that they do not endure through generations in society. Some staff take positive action on set occasions to select the gentler children, male and female, to play outside so that some of the dynamics of the group are addressed. The physically orientated children (who may be male or female) should also be given positive role models so that they feel positive about who they are. For example, children should see that it is fine to be female and enjoy being dirty and actively involved in making water wheels from old bike wheels and plastic cups.

'Providing support'

Potential of a puddle

Anning (1994) suggests that children know which activities are perceived as important through adult presence. When staff are in the outdoor learning area, they are more likely to be standing beside a climbing frame than a mud pie. Yet the learning is of equal importance.

'Talking through ideas'

Staff motivation should be addressed through ascertaining the 'motivational buttons' (Warden 2002) or interests of the adults. Many do not find bugs and beasties attractive, and it is their right not to.

However, more personally engaging aspects of work can usually be identified to find motivation. Once the whole curriculum is taken out of doors, it opens up scope for adults to support children in specific areas of the curriculum. Staff in some centres have analysed the skills within their teams, and different staff have gone on to take responsibility for developing lines of progression into transient art, the imaginative worlds of the 'little folk', weaving with natural materials, building dens or technology (e.g. moving water). Most of these cross over traditional methods of planning curricular content.

Sustainable projects and methods of working are obviously the most beneficial. Many establishments have created outdoor areas primarily through the motivation of one or two key people. When these key people move elsewhere, outdoor areas sometimes decline in both their use and maintenance. The development of an effective outdoor area is a long-term commitment and should therefore be supported in policy and through continual professional development.

Sustainable purchasing comes through group commitment and support of the purchase. Resources will only be used over time if their

'Facilitating learning through provision of materials'

23

Sustain-
able
changes
and
develop
-ments

purpose and function are understood, and seen to be important to the learning process. Where staff motivation is low there can be a repetition of use of key resources, because all changes, no matter how small all require effort.

A self help system of any kind will need to be introduced to the children so that they

understand the use and potential of the resources. When children have been given a lot of adult direction and structure in their play, it can take some time before they will take back the ownership and autonomy of their play. Through our experiences most children engage in outdoor play within a short space of time if they feel the adult is supportive of the new behaviours. It is better for the changes to take place at a sustainable rate so that the quality gradually improves, rather than be superb for a couple of days and then non-existent the next week. Children need to able to

trust the provision so that they can plan ahead and develop a positive attitude to the outside space.

In order for adults to be knowledgeable and informed about outdoor learning we need to provide experiential training. In order for all adults to become motivated by outdoor play we need to find a way to inspire them. Our training takes into account learning styles of the adults we work with. Many people on the courses take home a positive attitude that then needs to be transferred into practice. This is often the hardest part!

A variety of approaches to training ensure that adults can access knowledge in a way that is appropriate for them. Internet courses,

websites, long term courses, practical skill days, conference days for whole staff teams, continuous development training programmes and centre based training are all available through companies such as Mindstretchers. Long term courses that drip-feed information at a rate that enables deep level learning are likely to lead to persistent change.

Potential of a puddle

The physical aspects of the outdoor area should be addressed creatively

Key points

·   Any outdoor space has the potential for learning.

·   An outdoor environment should be designed with children's behaviour and interests in mind.

·   Zones of learning can settle and focus children, although they should not be used in a way that prevents natural connections in learning.

·   Outdoor learning environments can be created using a few basic elements.

Outdoor play areas are busy places where the environment is used rather than admired; they are very different from a manicured garden. The involvement of the children in the creation and design of this space will provide the opportunity for greater ownership and a closer match between the children's needs and the provision.

Fisher (1996) argues that the most important question to ask is 'What do young learners need most?' and not to focus on the constraints of the environment. It may be that the children need large cardboard boxes and string to make a fishing boat. Commercial products do not always offer the most relevant learning.

Physical landscape

Large landscaping projects take time and can be very costly. Flexible resources and opportunities can be combined with basic elements of landscaping such as:

·   a variety of levels and gradients with slopes, dips and hollows
·   access to a range of textures such as hard surface, bark and grass
·   natural elements such as plants, trees, mud, water, rock
·   shelter, in a form that can be used in a variety of ways.

These four elements blend together to give environments that are full of discovery and potential for learning in all aspects of the curriculum.

'Hidden spaces, changing levels'

25

The basic landscape offers a framework that enables children to learn through the flexible use of resources.

These elements can be presented to children on a small scale through trolleys, large floor-based trays, guttering and a blanket and pegs; or on a larger scale through walk-in sand areas, woodland areas, babbling burns and willow domes. Every outdoor space has the potential to support learning.

'An oasis on the tarmac'

Many centres start with temporary bean arches that die back each year, before planting a permanent structure like a hazel or willow arbour. The advantage of more permanent areas is that they mature over time; the disadvantage is that they can become difficult for children to modify for use.

There are a number of key features of outdoor learning environments that practitioners often have concerns about.

Access

Access to the outdoor area
Ideally there should be a large door from the indoor play area to the outdoor play area, so that there can be a free flow of activity between the two spaces. This type of provision is positive and appropriate. However, for it to work on a day-to-day basis there has to be an underlying commitment from the adults in the environment to support and extend this movement.

Many centres have devised ways of easing the journey to the outdoor area, such as providing a rope to hold onto like a giant caterpillar, with gorgeous ribbons and bells tied to it; or temporary fencing to 'channel' the children across potentially hazardous areas, such as a main pathway running through the middle of the outdoor area.

One way of creating an interest in the outdoor environment is to give children the opportunity for decision making. Imagine the excitement of being a child and choosing how to get to the front door of the centre! Create two entry gates and a choice of pathways to get to the front door; each pathway could take a different route through the outside area, going

'Make the most of what you have'

26

under willow arches, over bridges, and around specially created mini-roundabouts. Experiencing a journey where you have the power to choose where you go is very different from just walking beside an adult and a pram. The importance of choice can be seen by the fact that many children love to walk around carrying objects for most of the day, yet they often flatly refuse to walk to the car!

Size and layout of the area
There is no perfect size for an outdoor play area, although most people would say that they want more!

A very large area offers its own challenges in terms of supervision, and a feeling of vulnerability in young children. Neill (1982) found that adults working in large open spaces spent more time overseeing, rather than interacting with, children in specific activities. Very large areas tend to be linked to nursery schools where up to a 100 children may have access to one area. There are a number of solutions to this, most involving division of the area. The space can be divided using a variety of means: bushes and shrubs in troughs, equipment trolleys, wooden poles, living walls, tyres, concrete blocks covered in mosaics, and temporary barriers made of fabric or wood. The space is usually subdivided into age-appropriate areas, curriculum zones or arbitrary spaces.

'Tyres to subdivide space'

Whichever option is chosen, the idea of different enclosures seems to give young children a sense of security, and many are more able to focus on learning.

However, we should take care not to subdivide and landscape outdoor areas too much, because this may remove children's choice and freedom and therefore take away some of their creativity.

Some centres have outdoor areas that are very small and far away from the main building. These areas have to be timetabled for small groups of children to use at different times so that children have enough space to move about. If the outside area is seen in combination with the indoor space then the majority of areas offer enough space to engage in high-quality learning.

'Child created dens'

The effectiveness of outdoor learning may be determined by what the team choose to put into the space they have. Bikes and wheeled toys can dominate areas, and many centres have dispensed with them on most days so that other physical skills and curricular learning can be developed. Very large climbing frames can be costly and invade the space. Blatchford (1989) suggests that purchasing outdoor climbing frames is not based on research but a perception that 'they are good to have'. Objects that allow children to design and build a structure in their own way offer better learning opportunities and better use of money than a single-use climbing frame.

Given the chance to start from the planning stage, the outdoor area should be large enough for there to be opportunities to have a feeling of being 'alone and independent' when a child wants to make a step away.

Creative seating

Shade, shelter and seating
Trees are a natural protection from wind, rain and sun, as well as a useful resource. Unfortunately many centres do not have trees, so alternatives should be considered. Shade is easier to create than wind breaks, and can be created using umbrella stands, erected pergolas, tipis, verandas, shop canopies and car port roofs. Children can also make dens using waterproof groundmats. Where centres are looking for more natural areas, then willow arbours can be planted with a series of tunnels leading into a central bay. This has a variety of uses, from a weaving frame, to a music area, to a role-play area.

The wind chill in Scotland is another factor: creating an area where the wind cannot whistle by to chill even the hardiest of children is a challenge that even trees find hard to fight! The most successful areas have been those that combine a short-term solution such as weaving fabric in and out of fencing (designed by children), along with a long-term goal of planting trees and shrubs, with a more solid structure such as a wall/strong fence.

One big difference between indoor and outdoor areas is often the lack of a settling place or seating. Staff and children should be able to settle in comfort somewhere in the outside area. This can be provided by something as simple as a plank and two crates, small groundsheets that children can put inside or out, or larger arbours or storytelling seats large enough for a group of people to gather on. In the Royal School of Dunkeld in Perthshire, the grounds have been developed to create an outdoor

Shade shelter seating

Potential of a puddle

classroom with seating provided in lengths of log with hollowed bowls for the seats. On a smaller scale, some centres have used a circle of logs, cross-sections of log, large boulders and traditional picnic tables.

Storage

Storage can also be an issue for some centres: either the amount of it or the location of it. Taking equipment outside can also cause difficulties. Many centres try to re-create the indoor environment outside by carrying large items in and out. Human nature is such that the motivation to do this will diminish on colder days when black clouds are gathering on the horizon! A more appropriate method would be to involve children in the process, by using trolleys or carry systems that can be pushed outside or hung onto the fence in a matter of moments, and then easily accessed by the children.

Structured outdoor resources should be available in the location of the activity. For example, provide role-play materials, paper, pens, maps, bundles of large keys, etc. near a secret den so that when children become involved in the activity they do not need to break away to go inside to fetch resources. A self-help system of bags of resources for children to choose from also works well.

Security and safety

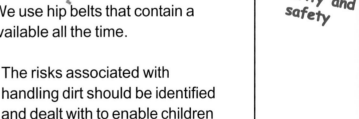

For staff to feel relaxed so that they can interact with children, there have to be secure boundaries and safe surfaces. Risk assessment is an integral part of the work we do, and we should be aware of it all the time. There will be checks to be made outside before children come to the centre, and care should be taken to ensure open areas of soil are free from faeces. Staff may want to consider how they manage objects such as scissors, first aid, communication with other staff when they are moving around the outdoor area. We use hip belts that contain a walkie talkie, notepad etc so that resources are available all the time.

Flexible storage that can offer resources to support the whole curriculum

The risks associated with handling dirt should be identified and dealt with to enable children to engage in messy play. Some centres create lidded pits or netted areas for digging zones; sand pits are available with lids that become seats; and there are mobile washing stands that enable the tidying-up process to take place outside.

Risk assessment

Each region in Scotland has a different form for risk assessment. Risk assessments are designed to encourage people to see hazards, so that they can act to reduce the possibility of injury. The responsibility to monitor them should belong to everyone, children included.

Balance challenge & risk

The procedure for risk assessments is the same across all regions. There is no one format that is the ideal. As with all forms, if the team design it, the thinking process becomes the most important element. We record risk assessments
- To show that a check was made
- To show that you considered who would be affected by the activity
- To demonstrate that the people involved have dealt with significant hazards
- To show that the precautions taken are *reasonable* and that the remaining risk is low.

The more risk assessments that we do the more secure we feel in our ability to work in a fluid environment outside. The process has been accused of being long winded and too paper based, in actual fact the benefits are far reaching. Through risk assessment the adult child interaction can be focussed on learning rather than safety, all people become involved, and ultimately accidents are reduced through preparation.

The procedure usually follows the following path; look for hazards; decide who may be harmed and why; evaluate the risks and decide whether precautions are adequate; record the findings in a usable format; review the assessment at regular intervals and revise it.

Each significant hazard should be considered in terms of the risk of it actually happening. That is high, medium or low probability. Health and Safety Education state 'Even after all precautions have been taken, some risk usually remains'. It is inappropriate to create play environments that are devoid of risk, to do that would reduce or even eliminate the learning potential. People do perceive the outside area as more 'risky', in actual fact it may be due to the open ended nature of play with natural materials that offer a greater challenge, since their use can be so varied and complex.

To gain examples of risk assessments it is possible to visit the British Countryside Trust Volunteers website, Forest Schools, R.O.S.P.A. All these organisations are involved in the maintenance of outdoor play environments that use risk assessments as part of the planning process.

Children can evaluate the risk

Potential of a puddle

Practitioners should be aware of the range of children's learning styles and preferences

Key points

· Outdoor spaces are the optimal learning environment for some children.

· All children have different learning styles, and practitioners can respond to these indoors and outdoors.

· Outdoor learning should be monitored to ensure that there is equal opportunity for all children to identify with aspects of their life and culture.

Children often demonstrate a change in behaviour when they move to the outdoor play area. This could be due to a subtle change in adult expectation when the play moves out of doors (Bilton 1998). The implicit understanding may well be that more noise, activity and freedom are 'allowed' out of doors. Alternatively, it could be that the atmosphere of working outside in a natural environment has a calming effect on children. The psychological effect of colour, light, shape and space has been established through research work on interior design and architecture (Dudek 2000). Green in all its variant forms is a positive colour; it is often missing in hard-surface outdoor spaces, and there are ways that practitioners can work alongside children to design and create areas that overcome this (Warden 1999).

Psychological effect

One clear advantage of an effective outdoor area is that it provides the opportunity for children to see and touch natural materials; we should therefore think carefully about how much plastic equipment to take into outdoor spaces, and whether such materials are necessary at all. Rather than selecting the brightly coloured manufactured resources readily available today, children often choose wooden books or natural pebbles to count with, or slices of wood to use as plates. Theorists such as Steiner, Montessori, and Froebel all supported the use of natural materials and forms to engage children because these allow them to focus on their own thinking and concept formation rather than be distracted by colour/pattern.

Natural materials

'Sensorial writing'

Expectations of the type and style of interaction between children is often different. Indoors there is often a greater emphasis on collaborative or group play; out of doors individual experiences and personal journeys are given greater scope. It would appear from talking to a wide range of early years practitioners that children are given more ownership in the play outside. This responsibility carries with it a higher degree of self-motivation and therefore individual focus.

'Feeling the sounds'

The staff planning is often more fluid out of doors, where children are encouraged to engage in epistemic 'play', discovering the opportunities of the area. In some centres there seem to be more directed or outcome-based activities indoors with less focused opportunities in the outdoor spaces. Giving children autonomy outdoors involves supporting choice and freedom. The focus is often there but comes from the child rather than the adult. It is to be hoped that adults see both indoor and outdoor areas of play as fluid and flexible so that children have ownership and are consulted throughout the learning environment.

There are many theories of play that try to make sense of the complicated and yet apparently simple process of playing. There is now a large amount of evidence that supports the idea that intelligence and learning are not fixed processes, but a network of different aspects that interweave to create a whole. Goleman (1995) put forward the idea that the development of emotional intelligence can be as important as other aspects of learning in terms of long-term development. The framework he puts forward includes self-awareness, management of emotions, self-motivation, handling relationships, and empathy. In an indoor–outdoor environment, these aspects are easily developed and then integrated into the methodology so that the approach is sustainable.

Self-awareness and the management of emotions are obviously affected by the environment that children play in. Bilton (1998) suggests four clear links between layout of the outdoor play area and the way that these areas are used by children:
· overcrowding can affect children and cause aggression
· being given uninterrupted time to work will encourage children to persevere more
· in big open spaces, children can feel lost
· timetabling of the outdoor area can cause a number of behavioural problems.

Potential of a puddle

In an effective outdoor play environment the two spaces are seen as one working environment and can therefore provide more available space. In some very small outdoor spaces this has led to groups of children working outside for 1 hour blocks of time, supported by a key worker who enables the children's play focus to spread over a series of days.

Large spaces can be subdivided to respond to children's need for enclosure. The dividers appear to be most effective when they are mobile so that the environment can be altered on a day-to-day basis.

In some centres the fluid nature of play is becoming disturbed by structured sessions of activities. If children know that they have only 15 minutes outdoors they will not bother to persevere with tasks or even start to embark on them. It takes a while to plan and build a structure. Some of the behaviours we see children demonstrate are developmentally appropriate, such as transporting stones, filling and emptying buckets with mud, enclosing and enveloping plastic beetles in large leaves. In fact, rather than preventing and controlling these behaviours, they should become motivational buttons that we can use to plan children's learning (Warden 1999). Our skill as practitioners is to consider to what extent children's behaviours are caused by our provision.

'Collecting & gathering' schema

The schemas outlined below are the most common and children may flow in and out of schema over time. Schemas are evident across all the curricula boundaries and are perhaps a more child-centred way of planning and responding to children.

Transporting
Here and there:- looking from where you are to over there (variety of tools such as binoculars/lens/diffraction tube), putting up pulley systems to move objects from here to there and back again, bags and containers to carry objects in.

Going through a boundary
Going through:- Pooh sticks, stepping through gaps and holes, walking through a wood.
Going over:- climbing over logs, stepping over streams, bridges.
Going under:- arches, holes in walls. Walking under low branches, under cloths.
Going around a boundary:- walking around a tree, weaving ribbons around a tree or an area. Interest in fences, boundaries, walls.

Circularity
Circles of wood, cross sections. Going round and round in a space.
Weaving grasses into hoops, rings.

Holes in leaves.
Holes in the ground by worms, rabbit holes, etc.
Poking holes in the mud with a stick.
Peering through holes to see the view.

Rotation/spiralling
Spiral forms such as rolled up ferns, spirals on a snail shell.
Spirals drawn on hard surface.
Twisted vines e.g. Honeysuckle.
Watching wind spiral up the leaves on a windy day.

Enclosing and enveloping
Collecting objects into pockets, pouches.
Wrapping stones in leaves.
Making holes and hiding plastic animals in them.
Wrapping themselves in clothes, coats, gloves.
Hiding inside boxes, dens, spaces.
Hiding objects under leaves, inside old logs.

Filling and emptying
Containers of a variety of sizes and shapes that are made by children.
Using man made containers to fill and empty a few yards away.
Access to water, soil, leaves, fire bricks, etc to put into the containers.
Pockets and pouches to carry around.

Connecting
Lining up sticks, long grasses, leaves in rows both vertical and horizontal.
Connecting objects to build dens, shelters.
Making links between bikes, boats, cardboard boxes.
Threading daisy chains.
Making circular wreaths from grass.
Using willow to weave, twist and connect.
Holding hands, making rings.
Using a variety of natural objects to push into holes, connecting many objects to one (see above).

Self-motivation is more likely to develop in environments where personal achievement is supported through praise rather than extrinsic rewards. The effective outdoor play area is a self-fulfilling environment that often offers a greater sense of autonomy and therefore self-gratification. The choice of what to play with should be in the hands of the children, and the location of the play can be flexible given a degree of space. Resources should be freely available, chosen and used in flexible ways: for example, grass for the walls of a house, flowers for soup, etc. And in environments that are based on indoor–outdoor planning the children can choose which space to be in and for how long.

Potential of a puddle

Developing relationships and a sense of empathy is a challenge for many very young children. Creating spaces where children of different age groups can play is a natural environment for learning about the dynamics of relationships. Some centres have subdivided their space for different age groups; others have left the space wide open to encourage children to play together. These nurseries have limited the use of bikes so that some days are bike free. When the bikes are used, they have a collaborative role being used as wagons, taxis and chariots, or perhaps an imaginative role as the 'dog warden's collecting van', or McDonalds drive-through. If children are using bikes they should be in a defined area with clear objectives rather than merely blowing off steam. The learning that takes place on a bike can be developed in other ways, and removing the bikes may affect the atmosphere and purpose of the outdoor area in a positive way.

The role of bike play

Another aspect of learning styles has been linked to Howard Gardener's theory of multiple intelligences (1993;1999). Gardener suggests that we need to look beyond traditional forms of IQ such as linguistic and mathematical learning to a broader view that enables all people to celebrate their own intelligence. To this end he defines eight intelligences that include linguistic, logical-mathematical, musical, bodily kinaesthetic, spatial, interpersonal, intrapersonal and naturalist. The bodily kinaesthetic learners are adept at learning through movement. We should be looking at the way that all children use their whole bodies to engage in learning in a physical and interactive way. The outdoor area provides an area

Multiple intelligences

'Resources to encourage movement'

that lends itself to physical learning. Children and adults have the opportunity to be involved in large scale learning, whether with real bricks and logs, or perhaps den building with branches and fabric.

The outdoor learning environment should be seen to be a parallel or complementary place to learn, with the whole curriculum on offer, so that each child is given the opportunity to develop aspects of their intelligence. The materials that we use to support children may well be different. In a natural outdoor area there will be sensory materials to use to make up stories to tell, count with, arrange into a transient picture, measure out to make some mud soup, draw pictures with; or there will be mini beasts to study. There will be a landscape and resources that encourage children to move and learn all aspects of the curriculum on the go, to enable them to make maps, and design and create areas full of sound and rhythm with logs and drum sticks. There will be the

Cross curricular experiences

35

chance to sit in a willow den that you have made yourself, to talk and care for other people with you, while learning all about the outdoor space around you, whether it is urban or rural. In short, there should be something for everyone.

Multi-cultural learning

Multi-cultural learning is not a single series of events; it is a way of living that will affect all of the children in your care. Looking at the way that the outdoor space reflects a multi-cultural society can lead to exciting and dynamic ideas. Cultural forms of art such as mosaics, and architectural shapes such as domes and spires, can be incorporated into the design. Creation of dwellings such as yurts and tipis can provide first-hand experience of people with a lifestyle that closely connects with nature. Cultural perspectives on Outdoor Learning nee to be discussed and taken into account throughout the process.

Partnership of community and centre

Any outdoor space offers opportunities for play. If children play in built-up areas with tarmac and concrete when they are not at the centre it can be more beneficial to enter their world and present opportunities that can be repeated in social play outside centre hours. No outdoor environment should be presented as the 'best' or only way. The attitude of the practitioners should support community and home, through subtle ways so that children can transfer experiences between centre and community. Community and street play has been studied over the years. Many people have clear memories of 'community games' or places to go. Projects based in schools are encouraging children to create their own community culture for outdoor play.

Equality of opportunity

Equality of opportunity can manifest itself in subtle ways. For example, the effect of children's clothing has a marked effect on the type and quality of play. Bilton (1998) examines the gender imbalance in outdoor play areas through the research of Tizard (1976), Hart (1978) and Cullen (1993). These studies suggest that there are clear examples of the dominance of one group, mainly male. Hart's research suggests that boys use the area to construct pretend houses whereas girls create the décor and detail. Where girls had started to build something, the boys often took over and the play was re-directed. In fact, it may well go beyond gender to emotional dominance, with more assertive, physically orientated children, boys or girls, directing constructive or active aspects of outdoor play. The practitioner's role is to observe these behaviours, offer a range of experiences outdoors that support equality of opportunity and if necessary take positive action to re-dress the imbalance.

Potential of a puddle

Staff should develop a policy so that they have a common understanding of, and a consistent approach to, outdoor learning

Key points

· An outdoor play policy should be created by the team working in the centre.

· The policy should be of use to staff, parents and visitors.

· The policy should affect practice.

Every centre has a unique way of developing its outdoor play area. The landscaping of the area and the acquisition of resources are only the first step. For the outdoor learning environment to work effectively, the methodology and management of the area have to be developed by the team.

In developing a policy, many discussions will have to take place so that the team can share views and come to a common understanding about the role of outdoor

'Consulting children about the outdoor provision'

learning in their centre. The development of outdoor play areas is now a priority in many parts of Scotland. When the diggers have moved away, and the children start to use the area, it will take some time for the atmosphere to settle into one of purposeful play. The staff role at this point will be to create a framework that promotes ways of working. This could include consultation with children by using talking and thinking books; self-help schemes for resource management; routines and expectations. If the staff have developed a draft policy they can then revisit it to refine and adapt it in response to observations. Without a policy, the staff role can become ill defined and the provision fragmented.

The questions in the table that follows are designed to support staff in a reflective process, so that they can consider some of the key features and principles outlined in this document in relation to their own specific outdoor environments.

The outdoor policy is the start of a process that leads to effective outdoor play. It should be revisited and used so that it influences practice. Avoiding jargon ensures that it will be accessible to everyone and therefore more likely to influence new possibilities.

Group ownership

Creation of a joint approach

Areas of content	Questions to discuss
Rationale Aims (broad) Objectives (detail)	Why do you feel outdoor play is important? Why are you encouraging children to go out? What references are there to outdoor play in the curriculum documents?
Time	How often would you like children to be outside? How long do you feel they should be outside? 15 minutes? 60 minutes? All morning? To what extent should children be outside throughout the year?
Weather	What preparations will you make for rainy, cold, hot weather? Will children be allowed to go out in poor weather?
Curriculum	Which aspects of the curriculum do you wish to cover when you are outside?
Planning	How will your planning link indoor and outdoor learning? How will you consult children about their plans or ideas?
Observation	What system will you use for observations outdoors?
Methodology/ organisation of resources	How will the staff make sure that there is self-selection and choice outdoors? How will staff involve children in setting out equipment?
Adult role	What will adults be expected to do when they are outside?
Risk assessment, vandalism, safety	Who will monitor the safety of the ground/equipment? How will equipment be stored?

© Claire Warden 2005

Mind Stretchers

Outdoor Play Policy
To be read in conjunction with other curriculum policies.

Rationale

Children should enjoy energetic activity both indoors and out and the feeling of well being that it brings. Outdoor play provides a multi-sensory environment which responds to individual learning styles. It complements and enhances all aspects of children's development and learning through its physical, open ended nature.

Aims

To create opportunities to explore outdoor environments.

Objectives

To enjoy outdoor activity throughout the seasons.
To investigate and experiment with a variety of natural resources.
To make discoveries using senses.
To use language to describe, explain, predict, ask questions and develop ideas.
To develop an appreciation of natural beauty and sense of wonder.
To care for personal safety.
To care for the environment of the centre, and create an awareness of wider issues.

Implementation

In order for this policy to be implemented in the centre, the staff will;
Provide resources that allow children to self select.
Present resources in a stimulating manner.
Provide resources that cover all aspects of the curriculum.
Dress children appropriately for all weather conditions.
Interact with children to extend learning.
Model a positive attitude to outdoor play.
Ensure outdoor area is adequate, safe and secure.
Raise parental awareness of the benefits of outdoor play.
Encourage parental involvement in outdoor activities.
Encourage opportunities started in nursery to be extended into the home environment.
Provide resources from outdoors in nursery.
Endeavour to provide outdoor activity every day (if possible).
Plan in responsive ways to ensure continuation on indoor/outdoor.
Make observation in the outdoor area.

Review date.

Potential of a puddle

Conclusion

Learning in an outdoor environment should be an integral part of an early years provision.

Practitioners should look at the potential of whatever space they have outdoors and consider how they can extend its use. No one element is absolutely necessary: for example, large areas of grass are not always necessary. Children can work with a square metre of grass, barley and corn set into paving slabs, and still gain from the sensory experiences and wonderful learning opportunities.

People are creative thinkers and this ability starts in childhood. Children are the greatest designers of outdoor space because they hold no preconceptions about what it should be like. Involvement of children in the planning, design and use of the area will create a more effective match between the provision and children's need.

Planning should reflect a flow of ideas and resources from an indoor environment to outdoors. The way that the information is recorded will vary between centres but the concept should remain the same.

The way that people learn varies according to their learning style and preferences. There are a group of children in our centres that will not be stimulated if we merely provide indoor learning. The use of multi-sensory resources will engage a wider range of learners in any area of the curriculum, both indoors and outdoors.

Practitioners are the decision makers at the initial stages of outdoor play development. If there is a real motivation to take children outdoors, then many practitioners can achieve great things, even from small tarmac environments. Where there is a will there is a way!

1 Whiting Bay Playgroup, Isle of Arran, North Ayrshire

Whiting Bay Playgroup is based in a small church hall. The group have permanent use of the hall, but the outdoor play area is part of the church grounds and has to be cleared every day. The area is surrounded by a hedge and the wall of the church; the surface is grass. There is a door from the playroom leading directly outside. Cloakroom and toilets are in another part of the building. The outdoor play area is used by the children on a daily basis; there is access on most days for the majority of the session.

The observation and audit process identified the following points for development:

· provide curricular resources for outdoor play, as an alternative to physical equipment
· acquire waterproof dungarees for year-round use, and provide a store near the door
· involve the local community in supplying resources, and in a parent rota.
· develop a storage area for self-help resources and more detailed resources.

The process of development was stimulated by training and support on outdoor learning and the enthusiasm of the practitioner to see potential in simple affordable resources.

'Textured weaving '

Larger resources such as cardboard boxes and construction sets are set up by the adults before the children come outside. The smaller resources are provided in a series of woven baskets on groundsheets or through a self-help bag system. Resources are open-ended and have led to children creating things in imaginative ways, including textured weaving.
The area has been subdivided into areas related to the physical features such as trees, sculptures and walls. The area is small so, although there are defined settling areas, most of the curriculum is offered in a holistic way that is a balance of adult-initiated and child-led opportunities.

The creative area is positioned next to a tree, making use of the branches to hang wind-chimes and wind-socks. The children have created home-made instruments from metal tubing, sticks, CDs, recycled plastic bottles, etc. The groundsheet has pockets in it to hide interesting sensory objects such as large bells or large gems for the children to find.

'Creative area'

The development of the creative area has increased the motivation of children who were not keen to play outdoors when the area offered purely physical/game-based opportunities. Children play a variety of objects from metal pans to tubular bells. Children of different ages are encouraged to play together in the same area.

'Sensory objects to hide and find'

There is a large sculpture in the outdoor area, which has been the stimulus for experimentation with structures and stability. The cardboard boxes are used frequently and, although they started out as blocks to build with, they are now used for hiding in, as dens or boats in role-play, and as truck containers to transport objects across the area. Children are encouraged to look around them when they build

towers. The relatively soft cardboard allows children to build structures much higher than would normally be possible with traditional wooden blocks.

'Creative use of open-ended resources'

The experimentation was extended through the use of ridged tubing, which was one of many resources supplied by the local community. A selection of balls with different weights and textures enabled children to focus on concepts such as sound, vibration, speed, support and balance. The tubes were rocked, laid down on the ground, held vertically, sat upon, shouted through ... the list goes on !

Investigating tubing and balls

Natural spaces are created by the trees and bushes. One particular area is underneath a large willow tree, children enclose themselves in its branches and peer out onto the other children in the area. The desire to hide behind the tree next to a hedge has led the staff to support this as a role play area. The availability of collectable objects such as leaves and twigs has

enabled children who enjoy carrying and transporting things to move objects in wheelbarrows to a variety of 'special places'. Staff have supported this behaviour by introducing giant gems to move, numbers to collect and carry, letters to deliver.

Potential of a puddle

The need for waterproofs for use all year round was quickly identified. The high rainfall in Scotland ensures that children may be in damp spaces for most of the year; it is the ambient temperature that fluctuates! The provision of waterproof, durable dungarees was given a priority so that children could sit on damp grass, splash in puddles and crawl around in wet bushes throughout the year. Boots are provided by parents, since many children on the island spend time playing outside.

Adult support for the children is very evident - children are taken out every day, never mind the weather. One day in the nursery the children decided to make a rain shelter. The adults gave a variety of ribbon, yarns, string, pieces of fabric, pvc, builders plastic to select from. The children designed a large area of heavy duty plastic with holes punched around the outside edge. They attached wide variety of yarns to fly about in the wind. The wind factor proved to be a challenge, as the group moved outside the wind rose in strength to gale force. So much so, that the adults had to hold onto the rain shelter.

The effect of opening up an outdoor space has been to:
· double the available space to play
· offer an alternative area in which to learn – the physically orientated children are the first to move outside and often stay there most of the time
· widen the experiences of children to learn in a more sensorial way.

The points for development for the next stage will be to:
· continue the development of the area through resources and adult interaction to extend the involvement of children in planning through Talking and Thinking Books ©.

Potential of a puddle

Case study 2 - Morrisons Academy Nursery, Perth & Kinross

Morrisons Academy Nursery is based in the lower level of a large Victorian house, which has a large walled garden area at both front and back. The staff:child ratio is 1:7 and the nursery is in partnership with the region. The nursery is divided across three rooms organised according to the types of activity that take place; children and staff move freely between all rooms. There is a cloakroom/toilets at the back

Garden, 2002

door leading out into the back garden. Children are asked to bring wellington boots, outdoor clothing and a change of clothes. Most parents comply but there is spare equipment available just in case.

The outdoor area was identified through the development plan as an area that was not used to its full potential. The observations and audit process identified the following points for development:

·   create opportunities that cover the whole curriculum, to extend opportunities provided by the climbing frame currently available
·   extend time spent outdoors from 30 minutes in good weather to an hour or more in all weathers
·   introduce shelters to support all-weather use
·   include outdoor opportunities in planning that appeal to different learning styles
·   extend the storage system from adult-orientated to a self-help bag system for children to choose their own resources
·   introduce protective clothing for 'mud zone' or wet activities.

The outdoor area has been given additional funding, and staff have been highly motivated to extend the provision. It has been developed over a year to create the following opportunities.

Garden, 2003

Potential of a puddle

Areas of the garden are viewed as zones with linked activities, although the divisions are very flexible and are defined by practicality. The mud zone is offered in large tyres with protective aprons and has a low dividing fence to keep it as a separate area. The tree den and cooking area are included in this area, so that petal soup and mud Bolognaise can be on the menu.

A variety of creative activities take place in all areas outdoors: for example, weaving on wheels, painting on a perspex sheet permanently attached to the wall, transient art, watercolour palettes and materials to paint on, such as leaves, stones and bits of bark that are in the self-help bag system. Role-play and music happen across the area but are focused particularly in three den areas: a home area/house, a 'loft' (a covered area with hiding place below) and a natural den under the trees.

Mathematical activities are supported through materials in the bag system, such as tape measures, lengths of string and ribbon, jewels to hunt for, plastic bugs to find and sort.

Communication and language have been developed through the use of adult-led storytelling with the story apron, and the use of books in the 'loft' and all other areas of the garden.

Resources are sensory and linked to the children's interest. The adults provide materials through the self-help bag system, and a hanging area on the outside of the main store. Small groundsheets also hang here, for children to use where they like (these also double up as windproof sides for the den).

Physical play has been extended to be more flexible, for example there are tyres and planks to create an

'Sensorial resources'

obstacle course, climbing areas in the trees, large wooden building blocks to construct with, wings to dance with, dogs to take for walks, old canoes to sit in, a bike track to travel around in between den areas (materials such as postal hats are also on offer).

Scientific and technology-based activities take place across the area; there is a guttering run and washing line permanently set up to support experimentation and testing on

"Child planning"

an all-weather surface.

The washing line is used with a variety of materials such as ribbons, socks, wind-chimes to extend its use.

Planning sheets have been adjusted to take into account longer blocks of time in the outdoor area. The layout of the centre means that free flow access will be difficult to achieve, so longer blocks of time with clear indoor–outdoor learning links have been used to ensure continuity across sessions and learning (sample planning sheet).

Staff are flexible in their approach so that the numbers outside can change as children wish to move to a different environment. A member of staff has taken responsibility for overseeing the creation and development of the area so that there is a continuity of approach, although all members of the team are very positive and motivated to help.

The outdoor area is still in the process of development with identified targets for the next year already in place. The new action points include:
* planting more vegetation/perennial bushes such as willow, hazel, dogwood so that the materials can be used in play.
* negotiating with groundsmen to leave a small wild area with daisies, dandelions, long grasses, wood pile, bug mat, etc. for children to observe growth and life cycles of wild flowers and mini-beasts (there is an annual growing and planting area in tyres at the front of the centre).

Possible lines of development planning chart

Indoor interests and starting points

- Kn/w Overhead projector - offer lace, wool plastic spiders for children to explore light and shadow.

- Pd/m Hide bugs in sand pit - offer tweezers to pick them up with baskets to put them in.

- Cr/A Woodwork bench - offer wool and yarn alongside wood and nails.

- C/l Book area under table. Busy spider Incy Wincy and Storysack

Link to outdoor interests

- Weaving area provide string, ribbon and large spiders. Creation of own webs.

- Hide bugs in a variety of habitats. Provide grabbers, tongs etc.

- Den building area. Offer yarns and string to extend tying skills.

- Storytelling apron to be used in the willow area. Props to include spider, yarns, flies & twigs.

Next steps in learning

- Provide weaving frame (horizontal) to lie under.

- Hide bugs in appropriate habitats. Focus on camouflage.

- Provision of plant materials that can be used to lash and fasten.

- Stories to include different types of web building e.g. orb, funnel.

Case study 3 - Kildrum Nursery Centre, North Lanarkshire

Kildrum Nursery Centre is in a housing development in Cumbernauld. The centre has two areas that could be used for outdoor learning. Unfortunately the local area suffers heavily from vandalism, so the centre made the decision to focus on the smaller of the two outdoor areas, which is enclosed by the main building. There are 112 children on roll, which influenced the way this small area could be accessed. The nursery centre has a large area indoors. The outdoor area is poorly drained and can be very hot in the summer months. The vertical surfaces offered potential since the ground area was so limited.

The observation and audit process identified the following points for development:
· create an outdoor sensory area that could be used to develop all areas of the curriculum
· create an outdoor area that could extend key group planning
· involve children in the design and creation of the area.
· plan through child-initiated learning and interests.

Guttering was mounted on the wall; a digging area was created in an old paddling pool; a water barrel with a tap was installed for easy access to water; plants were put into narrow tubs.

In planning the outdoor area, the team at Kildrum follow the methodology of using 'talking and thinking' books with the children. The talking and thinking book provides a way of recording children's talk. A group of children are encouraged to speak about their ideas in a natural discussion (rather than in turn around a circle), and an adult scribes their comments. In Kildrum, each key group was encouraged to meet, talk and plan their ideas for the outdoor area. Each group took time to look at pictures of other areas, plants, colour charts, etc. so that they could have an informed discussion about what they wanted in their own outdoor area.

As is the practice with talking and thinking books, all the children's thinking was recorded through adult writing, and this was supplemented with children's drawings/writing, photographs and pictures cut from magazines.

The types of features that children want often vary from those of adults. One group wanted to build a tongue coming out of the wall, to put the 'eating plants' in. Another group wanted to hide squirrels, rabbits, moles and birds in the tree. Another group wanted to be able to plant carrots, have a path that could move every day, have some sunshine, a flower – and a tree just for Morven.

The most ambitious of the plans involved a den, which the group wanted to create. The key worker provided an old curtain and pegs and supported the group's wish to build a den around the tree. However, the curtain got wet and this stimulated discussion about more appropriate materials. The availability of a tarpaulin led the children to make a new roof. The den was used in that form for a week or so until an interest in Bob the Builder came through the talking and thinking books. Construction using hard materials was evident through the children's indoor play so the staff introduced large blocks, planks and tubing outdoors. It became evident from the children's play that they wanted to build a den that could 'stay up'.

The planning procedure started with rough sketches by individual children, to introduce the features that were important to them. The children wanted a chimney on the very top of the roof, a bird house at each side of the house, windows that they could open, a hole for a Christmas tree cable, seats, decoration and a carpet.

The wonderful aspect of this particular planning exercise is that the nursery had a link with a person who builds sheds and dens, so the children's ideas were able to become a reality. The wiggly circles and boxes that the children drew actually became the window shapes, and the chimney was built in exactly the place that the children wanted it. The children decorated logs slices with metallic

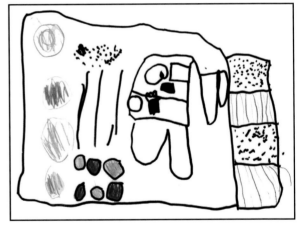

paint, and painted tiles to hang around inside the den. They helped to put carpet inside and created their own set of 'rules' for using the den:

Take your shoes off as soon as you come in so carpet doesn't get dirty
No hitting, no pushing, no kicking and punching
No silly words like bottom (!)
Be kind and listen

The children used the den for the two years that they were at nursery, each group developing and adding new details to it to make it their own. Unfortunately the tree in the outdoor area has had to be cut down because vandals used it to climb into the area, and a small fire they lit burnt some of the den. The children, who live locally, see this type of behaviour regularly and adjusted their play to include the 'time the den got burnt', as part of their role-play. The staff responded by putting in a pretend fire extinguisher.

The next steps for development are to invest in waterproof dungarees to extend the protection that nursery coats already offer; staff use their new wellingtons on a regular basis. The centre is moving towards making outdoor learning a daily opportunity.

These are some of the comments that the children made.
The comments were taken from the talking and thinking book and used as the focus for the design.

'Jake wants the den to have a roof, a door and a chimney (a birdhouse).'

'Dillon wants decorations inside like Santa's house. He said "I want tiles to paint on and a light".'

'Elaine wants the den to have wood and a stamper for everyone who listens, and a pen.'

'Grant wants decorations – silver ones – and balloons.'

'Caitlynn and Dillon want to make a Santa sign so he stops and leaves presents for them.'

'We need a wibbly window to see out'

Early Years Outdoors
Vision and Values for outdoor play

Since the completion of this book, the author has been involved in the creation of National Vision and Values. These are included here to support a consistent approach across the United Kingdom.

Vision and Values

The Vision for all young children

- All children have the right to experience and enjoy the essential and special nature of being outdoors.

- Young children thrive and their minds and bodies develop best when they have free access to stimulating outdoor environments for learning through play and real experiences.

- Knowledgeable and enthusiastic adults are crucial to unlocking the potential of outdoors.

Core Values for high quality outdoor experiences for young children

1. Young children should be outdoors as much as indoors and need a well-designed, well-organised, integrated indoor-outdoor environment, preferably with indoors and outdoors available simultaneously.

2. Play is the most important activity for young children outside.

3. Outdoor provision can, and must, offer young children experiences which have a lot of meaning to them and are led by the child.

4. Young children need all the adults around them to understand why outdoor play provision is essential for them, and adults who are committed and able to make its potential available to them.

5. The outdoor space and curriculum must harness the special nature of the outdoors, to offer children what the indoors cannot. This should be the focus for outdoor provision, complementing and extending provision indoors.

6. Outdoors should be a dynamic, flexible and versatile place where children can choose, create, change and be in charge of their play environment.

7. Young children must have a rich outdoor environment full of irresistible stimuli, contexts for play, exploration and talk, plenty of real experiences and contact with the natural world and with the community.

8. Young children should have long periods of time outside. They need to know that they can be outside every day, when they want to and that they can develop their ideas for play over time.

9. Young children need challenge and risk within a framework of security and safety. The outdoor environment lends itself to offering challenge, helping children learn how to be safe and to be aware of others.

10. Outdoor provision must support inclusion and meet the needs of individuals, offering a diverse range of play-based experiences. Young children should participate in decisions and actions affecting their outdoor play.

Rationale

We believe it is essential to underpin the Vision and in particular, the Values with a rationale for how this thinking came about, and more detailed information about what each Value means in reality. The additional details set out below reflect the thinking that took place and was recorded in the group sessions at the Vision and Values day on November 3rd 2003.

1. Young children should be outdoors as much as indoors and need a well-designed, well-organised, integrated indoor-outdoor environment, preferably with indoors and outdoors available simultaneously.

Outdoor provision is an essential part of the child's daily environment and life, not an option or an extra. Each half of the indoor-outdoor environment offers significantly different, but complementary, experiences and ways of being to young children. They should be available simultaneously and be experienced in a joined-up way, with each being given equal status and attention for their contribution to young children's well-being, health, stimulation and all areas of development.

Outdoor space must be considered a necessary part of an early years environment, be well thought through and well organised to maximise its value and usability by children and adults, and design and planning must support developmentally appropriate practice, being driven by children's interests and needs.

2. Play is the most important activity for young children outside.

Play is the means through which children find stimulation, well-being and happiness, and is the means through which they grow physically, intellectually and emotionally. Play is the most important thing for children to do outside and the most relevant way of offering learning outdoors. The outdoor environment is very well suited to meeting children's needs for all types of play, building upon first-hand experiences.

3. Outdoor provision can, and must, offer young children experiences which have a lot of meaning to them and are led by the child.

Because of the freedom the outdoors offers to move on a large scale, to be active, noisy and messy and to use all their senses with their whole body, young children engage in the way they most need to explore, make sense of life and express their feeling and ideas. Many young children relate much more strongly to learning offered outdoors rather than indoors.

All areas of learning must be offered through a wide range of holistic experiences, both active and calm, which make the most of what the outdoors has to offer.

Outdoor provision needs to be organised so that children are stimulated, and able, to follow their own interests and needs through play-based activity, giving them independence, self-organisation, participation and empowerment. The adult role is crucial in achieving this effectively.

4. Young children need all the adults around them to understand why outdoor play provision is essential for them, and adults who are committed and able to make its potential available to them.

Young children need practitioners who value and enjoy the outdoors themselves, see the potential and consequences it has for young children's well-being and development, and want to be outside with them. Attitude, understanding, commitment and positive thinking are important, as well as the skills to make the best use of what the outdoors has to offer and to effectively support child-led learning; the adult role outdoors must be as deeply considered as that indoors. Practitioners must be able to recognise, capture and share children's learning outdoors with parents and other people working with the child, so that they too become enthused. Cultural differences in attitude to the outdoors need to be understood and worked with sensitively to reach the best outcomes for children.

5. The outdoor space and curriculum must harness the special nature of the outdoors, to offer children what the indoors cannot. This should be the focus for outdoor provision, complementing and extending provision indoors.

The outdoors offers young children essential experiences vital to their well-being, health and development in all areas. Children who miss these experiences are significantly deprived.

Outdoors, children can have the freedom to explore different ways of 'being', feeling, behaving and interacting; they have space -physical (up as well as sideways), mental and emotional; they have room and permission to be active, interactive, messy, noisy and work on a large scale; they may feel less controlled by adults.

The real contact with the elements, seasons and the natural world, the range of perspectives, sensations and environments - multi-dimensional and multi-sensory, and the daily change, uncertainty, surprise and excitement all contribute to the desire young children have to be outside. It cannot be the same indoors, a child cannot *be* the same indoors - outdoors is a vital, special and deeply engaging place for young children.

6. Outdoors should be a dynamic, flexible and versatile place where children can choose, create, change and be in charge of their play environment.

Outdoor provision can, and should, offer young children an endlessly versatile, changeable and responsive environment for all types of play where they can manipulate, create, control and modify. This offers a huge sense of freedom, which is not readily available indoors. It also underpins the development of creativity and the dispositions for learning. The space itself as well as resources, layout, planning and routines all need to be versatile, open-ended and flexible to maximise their value to the child.

7. Young children must have a rich outdoor environment full of irresistible stimuli, contexts for play, exploration and talk, plenty of real experiences and contact with the natural world and with the community.

Through outdoor play, young children can learn the skills of social interaction and friendship, care for living things and their environment, be curious and fascinated, experience awe, wonder and joy and become 'lost in the experience'. They can satisfy their deep urge to explore, experiment and understand and become aware of their community and locality, thus developing a sense of connection to the physical, natural and human world.

A particular strength of outdoor provision is that it offers children many opportunities to experience the real world, have first-hand experiences, do real tasks and do what adults do, including being involved in the care of the outdoor space. Settings should make the most of this aspect, with connected play opportunities.

An aesthetic awareness of and emotional link to the non-constructed or controlled, multi-sensory and multi-dimensional natural world is a crucial component of human well-being, and increasingly absent in young children's lives. The richness of cultural diversity is an important part of our everyday world; this can and should be explored by children through outdoor experiences. Giving children a sense of belonging to something bigger than the immediate family or setting lays foundations for living as a community.

8. **Young children should have long periods of time outside. They need to know that they can be outside every day, when they want to and that they can develop their ideas for play over time.**

High quality play outdoors, where children are deeply involved, only emerges when they know they are not hurried. They need to have time to develop their use of spaces and resources and uninterrupted time to develop their play ideas, or to construct a place and then play in it or to get into problem-solving on a big scale. They need to be able to return to projects again and again until 'finished' with them.

Slow learning is good learning, giving time for assimilation. When children can move between indoors and outside, their play or explorations develop further still. Young children also need time (and places) to daydream, look on or simply relax outside.

9. **Young children need challenge and risk within a framework of security and safety. The outdoor environment lends itself to offering challenge, helping children learn how to be safe and to be aware of others.**

Children are seriously disadvantaged if they do not learn how to approach and manage physical and emotional risk. They can become either timid or reckless, or be unable to cope with consequences. Young children need to be able to set and meet their own challenges, become aware of their limits and push their abilities (at their own pace), be prepared to make mistakes, and experience the pleasure of

Potential of a puddle

feeling capable and competent. Challenge and its associated risk are vital for this. Young children also need to learn how to recognise and manage risk as life-skills, so as to become able to act safely, for themselves and others.

Safety of young children outdoors is paramount and a culture of 'risk assessment to enable' that permeates every aspect of outdoor provision is vital for all settings. Young children also need to feel secure, nurtured and valued outdoors. This includes clear behavioural boundaries (using rules to enable freedom), nurturing places and times outside and respect for how individual children prefer to play and learn.

10. **Outdoor provision must support inclusion and meet the needs of individuals, offering a diverse range of play-based experiences. Young children should participate in decisions and actions affecting their outdoor play.**

Provision for learning outdoors is responsive to the needs of very active learners, those who need sensory or language stimulation and those who need space away from others – it makes provision more inclusive and is a vital learning environment. When children's learning styles are valued, their self-image benefits. Boys, who tend to use active learning modes more than girls and until they are older, are particularly disadvantaged by limited outdoor play.

All children need full access to provision outdoors and it is important to know and meet the needs and interests of each child as an individual. Young children react differently to the spaces and experiences available or created so awareness and flexibility are key to the adult role. Observation and assessment (formative and summative), and intervention for particular support, must be carried out outside. While it is important to ensure the safety of all children, it is equally important to ensure all are sufficiently challenged.

Young children should take an active part in decisions and actions for outdoor provision, big and small. Their perspectives and views are critical and must be sought, and they can take an active role in setting up, clearing away and caring for the outdoor space.

The Vision and Values Partnership

The 'Early Years Outdoors' Vision and Values have been developed by a group specially convened for the purpose. This group includes:

- Bexley EYDCP
- British Association for Early Childhood Education (Early Education)
- Diane Rich, Rich Learning Opportunities
- Early Childhood Forum
- ESTYN (HMI Education and Training in Wales)
- ESIS (Wales)
- Grounds for Learning
- Helen Bilton, author and consultant
- Integrated Inspection Scotland
- Kent EYDCP
- Learning through Landscapes
- Margaret Edgington, author and consultant
- Marjorie Ouvry, author and consultant
- Claire Warden, author and consultant Mindstretchers (Scotland)
- National Assembly for Wales
- National Day Nurseries Association
- Neath Port Talbot LEA
- Paddy Beels, Wingate Nursery School
- Pre-school Learning Alliance
- Sightlines Initiative
- Stirling Council
- Sue Humphries, author and consultant
- Thomas Coram Institute
- West Sussex EYDCP

Potential of a puddle

Suppliers/Contacts

Equipment suppliers	Points of interest
Community Playthings Robertsbridge, East Sussex, TN32 5DR	Excellent trikes/bikes Baby wagon
Eco Schools Islay House, Livilands Lane, Stirling FK8 2BG	Charity set up to promote ecological issues in education
Eibe Play Eibe House, Home Farm, Hurtmore, Godalming, Surrey, GU8 6AD	Wonderful ideas, things to save up for
Forest Schools Gordon Woodall www.forestschools.com	Forest School training and development
Forestry Commission Sally York www.forestrcommission.gov.uk/scotland	Support for the development of Forest Schools - Scotland
Scottish Natural Heritage Battleby, Redgorton, Perth PH1 3EW	Raising Awareness of the Natural Heritage
C.J. Wildbird Foods The Rea, Upton Magna	Wide range of feeders, bird foods & nest boxes
Mindstretchers The Warehouse, Rossie Place, Auchterarder, Perthshire PH3 1AJ www.mindstretchers.co.uk	Curriculum support & training, indoor and outdoor educational resources. Articles & newsletter
Grounds for Learning, Stirling University (Scottish section of Learning Through Landscapes) - www.gflscotland.org.uk	Curriculum support & advice
Scottish Wildlife Trust Cramond House, Cramond Glebe Road Edinburgh EH4 6NS	Curriculum support & advice
Organic Gardening Ryton-on-Dunsmore Coventry CV8 3LG	Organic gardening advice
Wildflower Nursery Jupiter Urban Wildlife Centre Wood Street, Grangemouth FK3 8LH	Variety of native wildflowers
BTCV Scotland Balhallan House, 24 Allan Park Stirling FK82QG 01786 479697	Practical environmental education. "Learning through doing"

scotland@btcv.org.uk or www.btcv.org.uk

Bibliography

Anning, A. (1994) *Play and Legislated Curriculum: Back to basics*.

Athey, C. (1990) *Extending Thought in Young Children: A Parent-Teacher Partnership.* London: Paul Chapman Publishing

Bartholemew, L. (1996) 'Working in a team', in Robson, S. and Smedley, S. (eds.) *Education in Early Childhood*. London: David Fulton Publishers, pp. 4–55

Bilton, H. (1989) 'The Development and Significance of the Nursery Garden and Outdoor Play,. unpublished MA dissertation, University of Surrey

Bilton, H. (1993) 'The nursery class garden – problems associated with working in the outdoor environment and possible solutions', *Early Child Development and Care* **93**, 15–33

Bilton, H. (1994) 'The nursery class garden: designing and building an outdoor environment for young children', *Early Years* **14**(2), 34–7.

Bilton, H. (1998) *Outdoor Play in the Early Years – Management and Innovation.* London: David Fulton Publishers.

Blatchford, P. (1989) *Playtime in the Primary School. Problems & improvements.* Windsor Nelson

Bruce, T. (1987) *Early Childhood Education.* Hodder & Stoughton

Cole, E.S. (1990) 'An experience in Froebel's garden', *Childhood Education* **67**(1), 18–21

Cooper, M. and Johnson, A. (1991) *Poisonous Plants and Fungi - An Illustrated Guide.* London: HMSO.

Cullen, J. (1993) *Pre-school Childrens Use & Perceptions of Outdoor Play Areas.* ECD Care 89

Dudek, M. (2000) *Kindergarten Architecture* London: Chapman and Hall

Fisher, J. (1996) *Starting from the Child.* Buckingham: Open University Press

Filer. J. (1998) *Learning through Play – Outdoor Play*. Scholastic

Gardener, H. (1999)

Goleman, D. (1995) *Emotional Intelligence.*

Gura, P. (1992) *Exploring Learning.* London: Paul Chapman

Hart, R. (1978) *Differences in the use of Outdoor Space in Perspectives on Non Sexist Education* 101-9 New York Teachers College Press

Henniger, M.L. (1993/4) *'Enriching the outdoor play experience', Childhood Education* **5**, 87–90

McLean, S.V. (1991) *The Human Encounter.* Falmer Press

McNee, D. (1984) 'Outdoor play in the nursery – a neglected area?', *Early Years* **4**(2), 16–25

Miller, P. (1972) *Creative Outdoor Play Areas.* New Jersey: Prentice Hall

Moyles, J. (1992) *Organising for Learning in the Primary Classroom.* Buckingham O. U. Press

Nash, B. (1981) *Spatial Organisation.* B J of Ed Psychology **51,** 144-55

Naylor, H. (1985) 'Outdoor play and play equipment', *Early Child Development and Care* **19**, 109–30

Neill, S. (1982) *'Open plan or divided space'* Education **10,** 3-13

Ouvry, M. (2000) *Exercising Muscles and Minds - outdoor play and the early years curriculum.* NEYN

Ranzoni, P. (1973) *Considerations in developing an outside area for schools.* Orano: University of Maine.

Teets, S. (1985) in 'When Children Play' - Report from International Conference Assoc. of Educ.

Tizard, B. (1976) Play in Pre-School Centres. J of Ed Psychology **17,** 265

Tizard, B. (1977) 'Staff behaviour in Pre-school Centres' J of Ed Psychology **18**

Warden, C. (1999) 'Outdoor Play' - Mindstretchers

Warden, C. (2002) 'We-Go Outside' - Mindstretchers

Warden, C. (2005) Talking & Thinking Floorbooks - Mindstretchers

Yerkes, R. (1982) A playground that extends the classroom. London